Wired Minds

The Profound Impact of the Internet on Human Behavior

Jaxon Vale

DEDICATION

This book is dedicated to everyone who thinks that knowledge and creativity have the ability to change the world. To those who dare to envision a future in which technology and people coexist peacefully, and to the inquisitive minds that never stop asking questions and exploring new possibilities. I hope this piece encourages you to investigate, question, and build a society where advancement benefits everyone.

This book is a tribute to my family, friends, and mentors, whose unfailing encouragement and support have enabled me to take this trip. And to the readers who start this journey, I hope these pages will inspire and enlighten you.

You should read this book.

DISCLAIMER

This book's content is intended solely for educational and informational purposes. The author's research, experiences, and viewpoints are the foundation for the ideas, opinions, and suggestions presented here; they may not represent the opinions of any organization, entity, or person mentioned in the book.

Although every attempt has been taken to guarantee the correctness and dependability of the material provided, neither the author nor the publisher offer any guarantees or claims about the content's completeness, accuracy, or dependability. For specialized advice or help, readers are recommended to speak with professionals or specialists in related disciplines.

Both the publisher and the author disclaim all responsibility for any losses, damages, or outcomes that may result from using or interpreting the material in this book. Any decisions based on the information presented are entirely the reader's responsibility.

CONTENTS

ACKNOWLEDGMENTS

I want to express my sincere appreciation to everyone who helped make this book a reality. Without the assistance, inspiration, and knowledge of numerous people, this journey which has been one of development, discovery, and education would not have been feasible.

I want to start by expressing my gratitude to my family and friends for their constant conviction in my goal and support. Their love and understanding allowed me the space and inspiration I needed to finish this endeavor, and their encouragement kept me going when I was unsure.

I am immensely appreciative of the several experts, scholars, and influential people whose contributions shaped the concepts in this book. I am lucky to have benefited from their knowledge, as their research, ideas, and discoveries in the digital sphere have formed the basis for the subjects I study.

We are grateful to the mentors, editors, and beta readers who offered insightful criticism and helpful recommendations. Your suggestions enabled this book to take on its final form, guaranteeing that it is factual and interesting for readers.

Finally, I would like to express my gratitude to all of the readers who have decided to join me on this adventure. I hope this book helps you better comprehend the digital world and how it has a significant impact on our lives.

I am thankful to all of you who helped out in some manner; your combined efforts and knowledge have resulted in this book.

CHAPTER 1

A HISTORICAL PERSPECTIVE ON THE DIGITAL REVOLUTION

1.1 The Internet's Origins: From ARPANET to Worldwide Connectivity

We must first examine the internet's beginnings, which are based in academic cooperation and military research rather than business or entertainment, in order to comprehend its wide-ranging effects on humanity. The modern internet is the result of decades of adaptation, collaboration, and innovation. Its history starts in the late 1960s with the ARPANET project, which had far more modest goals but enormous ramifications.

During the Cold War, the US Department of Defense commissioned the Advanced Research Projects Agency Network (ARPANET) to enable safe and reliable communication between military and academic institutions. Although the system crashed after the first two letters of the word "LOGIN" "L" and "O" the first successful message between UCLA and Stanford was transmitted in 1969. Although it had a rough beginning, it was a pivotal moment.

Then came important technological turning points:

- Packet switching: a ground-breaking technique that divided data into smaller "packets" and transmitted them via various routes before reassembling them at the destination. Communications become more dependable and effective as a result.

- TCP/IP Protocols (Transmission Control Protocol/Internet Protocol): These protocols, which were standardized in 1983, made it possible for various networks to link with one another and served as the fundamental building blocks of the contemporary internet.

- Expanded usability was made possible by the Domain Name System (DNS), which was first introduced in 1984 and allowed users to enter memorable domain names rather than numeric IP addresses.

- The World Wide Web: Developed by Tim Berners-Lee in 1989 and made accessible to the general public in 1991, the web allowed for the creation of documents with hyperlinks, which allowed users to peruse information with relative ease.

As these technologies developed, what began as a specialized research tool quickly spread into corporations, academic institutions, and ultimately homes all over the world. The internet was emerging from technological obscurity into the public eye by the mid-1990s.

The development of the internet involved more than just a technological advancement; it involved a change in the way people interact, learn, work, and build relationships. It paved the way for a new era in which connectivity was more important than geography.

1.2 The Dot-Com Boom and Its Aftereffects

The internet had entered a new era by the mid-1990s, one that was fueled by media hype, entrepreneurial fervor, and the alluring prospect of limitless digital riches. This was the Dot-Com Boom, which lasted approximately from

1995 to 2000 and had a lasting impact on technical ecosystems, global economies, and cultural norms.

Companies whose domain names ended in ".com" and whose business models were largely centered on the internet are referred to as "dot-com." As the public's access to personal computers increased and user-friendly browsers like Netscape gained popularity, venture capitalists poured money into the IT industry. Startups appeared almost immediately, providing online services for everything from news and travel to banking and retail.

This era's distinguishing characteristics include:

- Hyperinflated Valuations: Based only on their potential for the future, companies with little to no revenue were valued in the billions.
- Massive Investment: Silicon Valley and other tech hotspots received billions of dollars in venture funding.
- Public Euphoria: During initial public offerings (IPOs), institutional and amateur investors rushed to purchase shares of internet-based businesses, resulting in an unsustainable bubble.

By the year 2000, however, it was impossible to overlook the faulty economics of many businesses. When the bubble burst, hundreds of businesses went bankrupt, losing trillions of dollars in market value.

The dot-com era wasn't a bust, though. It had significant long-term repercussions:

- The next digital wave would be powered by fiber-optic cables, data centers, and server technologies, all of which were heavily invested in due to the need of the time.
- E-commerce Foundations: Born during this time, Amazon and eBay not only survived but grew into titans.
- Digital Literacy: The public's usage of digital tools throughout this period prepared the way for their more advanced use today.

Trial and error was the norm during the dot-com boom. Though it also imparted hard lessons about scalability, sustainability, and speculation, it established the internet as a forum for creativity. Future digital endeavors' approaches to growth and governance would be influenced by the wounds of that time.

1.3 Web 2.0 Transition: Social Engagement and User-Generated Content

The emergence of Web 2.0 signified a significant shift toward interaction, cooperation, and involvement, if the early internet was a static, one-way digital bulletin board. Web 2.0, which was first used in the early 2000s, was a conceptual development rather than a complete technology redesign. Participatory platforms, networked communities, and user-generated content were highlighted.

Before Web 2.0, many people consumed material that was mostly produced by a small number of people. Web 2.0, however, made every user a potential publisher. This changed how people viewed their personal agency online as well as how they communicated.

Important developments during this time period included:

- Blogs and Wikis: Websites such as WordPress and

Wikipedia made it possible for regular people to produce, modify, and distribute information on a large scale.

- Social Media Platforms: Twitter (2006), YouTube (2005), and Facebook (2004) represented a new type of internet one in which discussions were instantaneous and worldwide.
- AJAX and Rich Web Applications: Made web interfaces more responsive and dynamic while facilitating more seamless user experiences.

Significant societal ramifications also resulted from this shift:

- Democratization of Information: Knowledge and opinions could be freely exchanged since they were no longer restricted by editors or organizations.
- Identity Formation: Individuals started creating online personas that shaped their social and professional perceptions.
- New Economies: Web 2.0 opened the door for new forms of employment and entrepreneurship, from gig workers to influencers.

But there were drawbacks to this interactive web as well:

- Misinformation and Echo Chambers: The same transparency that encouraged creativity also made it possible for lies to proliferate quickly.
- Data Ownership: By acquiring and profiting from the increased amount of content produced by users, platforms subtly amassed enormous influence.
- Mental Health Concerns: Users' psychological health started to suffer as a result of constant exposure to carefully manicured lives, online validation, and cyberbullying.

The internet was transformed from a tool to a dynamic, ever-evolving ecosystem by Web 2.0. The distinctions between creator and consumer, private and public, and fact and fiction were all muddled. And in the process, it changed what it means to be human in the digital age.

1.4 Internet Adoption: Worldwide Patterns and the Digital Divide

The internet's reach has increased dramatically with each

new technical development. Once a luxury of the West and elite institutions, it is now a basic commodity in many regions, much like clean water and electricity. However, the complexity of access increases along with connectivity, leading to the current digital divide.

The percentage of a population that has access to the internet is known as Internet penetration. Approximately 63% of the world's population, or more than 5 billion people, are online as of the early 2020s. However, the distribution of this access is far from equal.

Global internet adoption trends:
- High Penetration in Developed Nations: The United States, South Korea, and Norway are among the nations with internet connection rates above 90%.
- Rapid Growth in Developing Nations: Mobile technology is causing a sharp rise in connection in countries throughout Southeast Asia and Africa.
- Rural-Urban Disparities: Because of infrastructural issues, cities frequently have significantly better access than distant locations, even within nations.

The following factors influence the digital divide:

- Economic: For those with modest incomes, the cost of gadgets and data subscriptions may be prohibitive.
- Educational: Digital literacy is just as important as access; if you can't use the internet, you're not really connected.
- Political: Governments in some areas monitor or limit access to information.

The ramifications are profound and useful:

- Educational Gaps: In an increasingly connected environment, students who lack dependable internet are severely disadvantaged.
- Economic Inequality: Entrepreneurship and job prospects are restricted due to the inability to access digital markets.
- Civic Participation: People who are offline are not able to access important news sources, e-governance tools, or digital discourse.

Meanwhile, new developments are trying to close this gap:

- Low-Cost Smartphones and Data Plans: Making access more affordable in places with limited resources.
- Community Wi-Fi Projects: Local initiatives to provide internet access in rural areas and schools.
- The goal of initiatives like Starlink, which is a satellite internet project, is to provide broadband to even the most remote regions of the planet.

The internet has brought attention to and occasionally exacerbated pre-existing disparities, even as it has globalized the human experience. Closing the digital divide is now a social, economic, and ethical necessity rather than just a technical one.

The way people live, work, think, and connect has changed as a result of the digital revolution, which is a series of pivotal moments rather than a single event. The trajectory of the internet mirrors our own ambitious, imperfect, brilliant, and profoundly human from the military hallways of ARPANET to the private spheres of social media and online education.

Every stage of the development of the internet has brought forth new opportunities as well as obligations. We may better manage its current difficulties and imagine a more inclusive, moral, and empowered digital future if we have a greater understanding of this historical viewpoint

CHAPTER 2

Digital Age Communication

2.1 Transforming Human Communication Through Instant Messaging and Letters

Human civilization has always been held together by communication in its most basic form. Humans have always looked for quicker, clearer, and more effective ways to communicate ideas, feelings, and instructions—from prehistoric cave paintings to handwritten letters. But rather than merely speeding up this process, the digital age has completely changed it.

The Historical Transition from Paper to Pixels

Physical media had a major role in communication before the digital revolution. Days or weeks passed before letters arrived. In-person interactions were common, and landlines, specifically, provided real-time communication that was location-bound. With the advent of electronic mail (email) in the late 20th century, a significant shift occurred, offering the first taste of asynchronous, text-based digital communication that did not require physical transportation or co-presence.

Innovation exploded in the wake of this:

- Short Message Service (SMS) made it possible to communicate succinctly and in real time through mobile devices.
- Media sharing and continuous, real-time communication were made possible by Instant Messaging (IM) services such as AOL Instant Messenger, MSN Messenger, and later WhatsApp and Telegram.
- Geographical restrictions on meetings, distant business, and even family talks were removed by the advent of video conferencing platforms like Skype, Zoom, and Google Meet.

These changes reshaped expectations on availability, response time, and relationship maintenance in addition to speeding up communication.

The Culture of Constant On

People now anticipate prompt responses, which is a new form of social contract brought about by instant messaging. Traditional communication was asynchronous, which promoted introspection and deliberate expression. On the other hand, modern digital interactions promote speed, brevity, and frequent spontaneity. Although this promotes productivity, it also makes people more anxious about being available all the time, especially in work-related settings.

- Social pressure is increased by online status indicators and read receipts.
- Anticipatory communication loops are created via typing indicators.
- Push notifications bind users to their gadgets, frequently obfuscating the distinction between work and personal life.

This shift represents a major turning point in human

communication, one that prioritizes convenience and speed, occasionally at the price of nuance and purpose.

2.2 Social Media's Ascent and Its Social Consequences

What many refer to as the "social media era" began in the early 2000s. Social media sites like Facebook, Instagram, Twitter, and MySpace became societal phenomena rather than merely means for communication. By establishing virtual stages where people could curate identities, communicate with one another, and take part in international discussions, these platforms broadened the scope of human expression.

Making Communication More Democratic

Prior to social media, governments, news organizations, and publishing firms mainly regulated public conversation. Social platforms changed that dynamic entirely:

- Every individual got a voice, regardless of social class, region, or background.
- Viral campaigns, live-streamed events, and real-time

citizen reporting were made possible by the decentralization of news.

- From the Arab Spring to #BlackLivesMatter and #MeToo, social activism has found a home.

Both empowerment and accountability accompanied this democratization. It provided a voice to the voiceless, but it also fostered divisiveness, online harassment, and false information.

The Reality of Algorithms

Social media, in contrast to more conventional forms of communication, is controlled by algorithms that prioritize interaction over correctness or etiquette. Several consequences are introduced by this reality:

- As users are fed more of what they agree with via algorithms, echo chambers arise.
- Since emotionally charged information receives more clicks, sensationalism outperforms substance.
- Comparison culture thrives, causing anxiety, despair, and a warped perception of reality, especially in

teenagers.

The distinction between private and public life is also becoming increasingly hazy. Social media posts create a lasting digital footprint that frequently influences relationships and career prospects in ways that are not entirely apparent at the time of publishing.

2.3 Online Identity Formation and Virtual Communities

Community in physical locations is frequently characterized by geography, customs, or situation. These barriers are removed by the digital world, which enables people to connect with one another through common identities, passions, or experiences.

The Rise of Online Tribes

There are virtual communities in every possible field:

- Support groups for chronic illness, addiction, parenthood, and mental health.

- Fan communities centered on TV series, music, and novels.
- Professional networks that provide learning, collaboration, and mentorship.
- Niche forums such as Facebook groups, Discord servers, or Reddit.

A sense of belonging that is frequently absent from the real world is fostered by these communities. The internet can be the first safe place for people with stigmatized identities or unusual interests to express themselves authentically.

Building the Digital Identity

One's online persona is a carefully staged performance. People post romanticized images of themselves on social media. Users may choose usernames or avatars in forums or gaming settings to explore various aspects of their identities. This flexibility may be both complicated and freeing.

- Anonymity can promote both toxicity and honesty.
- Pseudonymity allows for experimentation and

role-playing.

- Pressure to uphold a particular image is created by hyper-curation, particularly among prominent personalities and influencers.

Offline reality and online identity are now intertwined. Companies look up job applicants on Google. Digital interactions are the foundation of relationships. There are real repercussions for one's online reputation.

2.4 The Decline of In-Person Interaction

Traditional human connection methods, particularly in-person interactions, are dwindling as digital communication becomes more widespread. There are costs associated with this change.

Social Skills Erosion

Young individuals who grew up with cellphones in their hands frequently express more uneasiness having face-to-face talks. The following issues are becoming more prevalent:

- The inability to keep eye contact.
- The inability to read nonverbal clues.
- Even in intimate partnerships, there is a preference for texting over talking.

Although digital fluency is a talent, interpersonal competency in the actual world shouldn't be sacrificed for it. Physical engagement is the primary means of developing soft skills such as empathy, active listening, and presence.

Dynamics at Work

The COVID-19 epidemic has boosted remote work, which has changed how people communicate professionally:

- Virtual meetings predominate, which limits chances for impromptu cooperation.
- Slack and Trello, two digital project management platforms, place more emphasis on task-oriented communication than on fostering relationships.
- As mentoring and onboarding grow more

transactional, workplace culture development is constrained.

Without the subtleties of face-to-face interactions, employee engagement and belonging frequently decline, even when productivity may stay high.

Close Relationships and Family

Screen time competes with quality time even in interpersonal relationships. According to studies, "phubbing," or ignoring someone in favor of a phone, can weaken parent-child ties and love relationships. Even when a device is not being utilized, its presence might make a conversation less in-depth.

Digital tools are not necessarily bad, to be sure. In actuality, they facilitate international cooperation, long-distance connections, and real-time connectivity between continents. Intentional usage is the main obstacle. The human element of communication runs the risk of being lost when digital becomes the norm.

In the digital age, communication is a complicated web of opportunity, innovation, and consequences. It has reshaped the limits of identity and expression, united disparate communities, and given voice to those voices. However, it has also brought about new kinds of depersonalization, distraction, and alienation.

Emotional intelligence, ethical awareness, and digital literacy are all necessary for navigating this environment. Instead of rejecting technology, the objective should be to humanize it so that we preserve the core of what it is to be human in our pursuit of connection.

CHAPTER 3

EMOTIONAL AND PSYCHOLOGICAL EFFECTS

3.1 The Causes, Signs, and Effects of Internet Addiction

The internet has changed from being a technological marvel to becoming an essential part of everyday life in the current digital landscape. It drives our enjoyment, facilitates communication, and is an essential tool for business and education. However, the potential of overdependence has increased along with its use, occasionally leading to what psychologists now call *internet addiction*. This is not just hyperbole or a catchphrase. There are real repercussions for mental, emotional, and even physical health from this quantifiable behavioral disorder.

Comprehending the Character of Internet Dependency

A compulsive drive to spend excessive amounts of time

online that interferes with basic living activities is known as internet addiction. Although not all psychiatric agencies have formally recognized it as a mental disorder yet (the DSM-5, for example, lists Internet Gaming Disorder as a condition that requires more research), mental health practitioners generally agree that it is a behavioral issue similar to other types of addiction.

The obsessive use may be focused on:

- Social media; streaming material; online gaming; pornography; continuous news consumption or browsing; and online gambling

Fundamental Reasons

Internet addiction is caused by a number of physiological, social, and psychological factors:

- Dopamine-driven reward loops: Likes, comments, and fresh content are just a few of the online behaviors that cause dopamine to be released, just like sweets or even narcotics do.

- Escapism: People frequently use the internet to escape uncomfortable feelings, obligations in real life, or social anxiety.
- Social reinforcement: Users are rewarded by digital platforms through feedback loops, such as algorithmic boosts, follower counts, and notifications, which can be addicting and seem validating.
- Lack of offline fulfillment: The immersive nature of the internet serves as a haven for people who are dissatisfied with their personal, academic, or professional lives.

Signs to Look for

Internet addiction can take many different forms, and it's critical to identify its signs:

- The inability to regulate internet usage
- Neglecting responsibilities at work, school, or home; lying about how much time was spent online; experiencing withdrawal symptoms (such as anger or anxiety) when not online; or experiencing

disturbed sleep patterns as a result of late-night gaming or browsing

- A declining offline life and social isolation

Extended Repercussions

Internet addiction can have a domino effect if left unchecked.

- Cognitive impairment: Prolonged stimulation can affect memory retention and attention spans.
- Mental health issues: An increase in depression, irritability, and anxiety is frequently noted.
- Physical effects: Musculoskeletal problems, sleep loss, eye strain, and obesity from sedentary lifestyles are common.
- Relationship strain: As people withdraw further into virtual worlds, their personal and professional relationships frequently suffer.

Addiction to the internet is more than just a lack of self-control. It must be handled with the same seriousness as other behavioral health issues because it frequently involves a complex interaction of social training, emotional need, and biological wiring.

3.2 Depression, Anxiety, and the Culture of Constant Connectivity

Once hailed as a victory of modern life, the idea of being constantly connected, always approachable, always updated was celebrated. Despite its convenience, this culture of constant communication has significantly harmed people's emotional health. Anxiety, sadness, and burnout are on the rise among people today, and many of these conditions are linked to the mental overload brought on by continuous digital exposure.

The Stress of Continually Being "On"

The lines between work and personal time have become more hazy due to modern technology. Social media gives the impression that everyone else is constantly "doing more" or "living better," while smartphones and email allow work to follow us well after office hours.

- It is now known that the psychological trigger known as "Fear of Missing Out (FOMO)" causes restlessness and discontent.

- Constant pings, alerts, and updates cause users to become "notice fatigued," which raises cortisol levels by keeping them in a low-level state of attention.

- Digital multitasking lowers attention span and leads to mental tiredness.

Social Monitoring and Anxiety

Social media frequently dictates our lives rather than just reflecting them. A subtle kind of social surveillance is created when we are aware that people are watching, like, commenting on, and judging our lives. This causes anxiety in a number of ways:

- Performance anxiety is the urge to always seem content or successful.

- Comparing oneself to others' carefully manicured online personas causes comparison anxiety.

- Anxiety about the quantity of likes or views a post

gets is known as validation anxiety.

Due to their developing self-concept and emotional control, adolescents and young adults are disproportionately affected by these influences. However, social media use is associated with higher levels of stress and discontent among adults as well.

Depressive Disorder in the Hyperconnected Age

Numerous studies have discovered connections between depressive symptoms and extensive internet use, although correlation does not equate to causation. Among the contributing elements are:

- Late-night scrolling causes sleep deprivation, which interferes with mood control.
- Disconnection from relationships in the actual world, which provide more emotional benefits than virtual ones.
- Exposure to bad content or global issues without the emotional tools to process them.

Algorithms also lack emotional neutrality. They frequently intensify emotionally charged material, such as anger, sorrow, and hopelessness, which exacerbates depression symptoms.

3.3 How Online Validation Affects Self-Esteem

People are social beings. It is in our nature to look for status, approval, and validation from our peers. This social dynamic has been digitalized by the internet, especially social media, which has transformed affirmation into quantifiable measures like likes, shares, comments, and follower counts. This can be reassuring, but it can also become quite addicting and closely linked to one's sense of value.

The Value Metrics

Twitter, Instagram, TikTok, and other platforms allow users to measure their level of popularity:

- More engagement or likes on a post make it seem more valuable.

- Having more followers might increase one's perceived desirability or credibility.
- Popular content is given priority by algorithms, which increases exposure for previously verified information.

This measurement frequently causes users to:

- An obsession with performance (e.g., the performance of a post).
- Feel rejected or disappointed when there is little engagement.
- Instead of relying on their own confidence, they base their sense of self-worth on digital validation.

Effects on Psychology

Emotional stability can be undermined in a number of ways by reliance on online validation:

- Externalized self-worth: Self-assurance is reliant on other people's responses.
- Inauthentic behavior: In an attempt to get likes or

approval, users may post things they don't really connect with.

- Mood fluctuations: Emotional states can rise or fall rapidly depending on digital feedback.
- Social comparison: Feelings of humiliation, envy, or inadequacy might arise when others are given more attention.

Adolescents and young adults, who are still developing their identities and are extremely sensitive to peer pressure, are most affected by this. Adults are not exempt, too, as influencers, professionals, and even corporations frequently link their perceived worth to digital performance.

3.4 The Road to Mental Resilience and Digital Detox

The practice of digital detoxification has become both necessary and a technique in response to these psychological demands. A digital detox is the deliberate reduction or cessation of internet-enabled gadget use for a predetermined amount of time in order to improve physical, mental, and emotional health.

The Resetting Science

By cutting off digital stimuli, the brain can revert to its more organic rhythm:

- Decreased cortisol levels: Less time spent around stressful situations.
- Better sleep cycles: Free from blue light and screen-induced mental stimulation.
- Improved creativity and focus: By removing outside distractions and promoting introspection.
- Emotional recalibration: By turning inward and away from external validation.

Useful Detox Techniques

- Scheduled breaks: Set aside specific times each day or each week to be offline.
- No-phone zones: Designate specific areas (dining room, bedroom) where electronics are not permitted.
- App limitations: Set usage limits using the built-in tools (such as Android's Digital Wellbeing or Apple's

Screen Time).

- Social media fasts: Take days or weeks off from social media on purpose.
- Mindful consumption: Before using the internet, consider why you are doing it. What am I hoping to acquire?

Establishing Durable Resilience

Giving up technology is not the goal of digital detoxification. Regaining agency and building resilience in a world that is constantly connected are the goals. To cultivate emotional and mental fortitude:

- Be mindful: Recognize how your ideas and emotions are impacted by digital experiences.
- Prioritize face-to-face interactions: Look for in-person interactions and discussions.
- Establish appropriate boundaries: Let friends and coworkers know when you expect to be available.
- Cultivate hobbies offline: Nature hikes, writing, exercise, and reading offer calming substitutes.

Instead of avoiding technology, the objective is to use it in a more purposeful and healthy way.

The effects of the digital age on the mind and emotions are a serious and pressing issue. The internet has many positive effects, but it also presents serious and hidden risks to our mental health. The issues that people face are very human and significant, ranging from the urge of addiction to the anxiety of continual contact and the empty pull of online validation.

We need to prioritize mental health, create boundaries, and approach our digital lives with mindfulness. Understanding the emotional dynamics at work gives us the ability to build better connections with our gadgets, our material, and eventually, ourselves

CHAPTER 4

CONSUMPTION OF EDUCATION AND KNOWLEDGE

4.1 The Internet as a Source of Powerful Information

The way we obtain, interact with, and share knowledge has been completely transformed by the internet. The digital world of today has democratized knowledge on a scale never before seen in human history, in contrast to the pre-digital period when academic institutions, libraries, and traditional media outlets dominated the flow of information.

Both significant and complex changes have occurred:

The concept of universal accessibility Internet connectivity provides access to a wide library of information, regardless of one's location a booming city or a secluded town. The information is as wide-ranging as it is varied, ranging from academic papers and textbooks to tutorials, videos, and discussion boards.

- A source of crowdsourced wisdom The communal contribution paradigm is demonstrated by websites such as Wikipedia, where knowledge is shared, edited, and improved by both specialists and laypeople. This model has accelerated the rate at which information is updated and made public, notwithstanding its shortcomings.

- Learning on Demand: Users can conduct research on any subject, from sourdough baking to quantum mechanics, with only a few keystrokes. The dynamic has changed from "search and wait" to "ask and know" due to this immediacy.

But there are drawbacks to the wealth of information as well:

- Overwhelming Information: Users frequently become overwhelmed by the abundance of information accessible and struggle to choose what is most accurate or relevant.

- Quality Variable: Not every source can be trusted. In this new knowledge economy, being able to distinguish peer-reviewed research from opinion pieces or pseudoscience is essential.

- However, one of the hallmarks of the digital age is the internet's ability to function as a source of knowledge. It serves as the foundation for the development and improvement of contemporary learning ecosystems.

4.2 The Future of Education and E-Learning Platforms

From a fringe project, e-learning has grown into a powerful force in international education. Cloud computing, high-speed internet, and mobile technology have all come together to create a vibrant ecosystem of online learning platforms that are changing the way that knowledge is disseminated and accessed.

Important Advancements in Online Education:

- MOOCs, or massively open online courses: Anyone with internet access can attend university-level courses through platforms like Coursera, edX, and Udacity. These platforms democratize higher education by collaborating with prestigious universities.

- Online Classrooms: Synchronous learning is now feasible at scale thanks to programs like Zoom, Google Meet, and Microsoft Teams. Real-time communication between students and teachers allows for immersive and engaging learning experiences.

- Online Certifications and Micro-Credentials: Multi-year degree programs are no longer mandatory for learners. People can upskill quickly and affordably with specialized credentials in fields like digital marketing, project management, or data science.

- Systems of Adaptive Learning: Many platforms now provide individualized learning routes that adapt in real time to the student's pace, skills, and limitations by utilizing artificial intelligence.

Online education has the following benefits:

- Adaptability: Students can interact with the material at their own speed, juggling their studies with obligations to their families, jobs, or other commitments.

- International Access: Economic and geographic obstacles are being lowered. Lectures from Stanford or MIT are now available to students in rural Kenya.

- Cost Efficiency: Online courses are frequently less expensive than traditional schooling, which lowers the cost of high-quality education.

Difficulties and Things to Think About:

Participation and Retention: Motivation is often a problem for online learners. MOOC dropout rates continue to be high because they lack the structure of regular classes.

- Digital Divide: For many communities, participation is still restricted by access to devices, internet connectivity, and digital literacy.

- Credential Acknowledgment: Although this is slowly improving, not all organizations or businesses give online credentials the same weight as traditional degrees.

E-learning's trend points to a mixed future in which digital and conventional approaches coexist. In order to improve engagement, interaction, and personalization, educational institutions are increasingly implementing blended learning methods, which combine in-person instruction with digital resources.

4.3 Fake news and misinformation: A challenge

The internet has made it easier to share knowledge, but it has also made it easier for false information to proliferate. The ease with which lies can be disseminated, circulated, and spread has detrimental effects on society's trust and ability to make educated decisions, in addition to education.

The origins and dissemination of false information:

- Social Media Virality: Sites such as Facebook, X (previously Twitter), and TikTok are designed to encourage interaction rather than precision. Compared to factual reporting, sensational or emotionally charged content frequently travels more quickly.

- Algorithmic Bias and Echo Chambers: Algorithms customize content according to user behavior, frequently confirming pre-existing opinions and forming echo chambers that protect users from opposing viewpoints.

- Content Manipulation: The sophistication of deepfakes, Photoshopped photos, and deceptive headlines is growing, making it more difficult to tell fact from fiction.

- Misinformation from Influencers: Misinformation can be purposefully or unintentionally disseminated by people with sizable fan bases, giving it legitimacy.

Effects on Society and Education:

The decline of trust: A climate of mistrust and divisiveness can result from the people losing faith in authorities, organizations, and education when false information spreads.

- Improper Choice Making: Misinformation can influence people to make decisions that are detrimental or against their best interests in a variety of areas, including politics and health.

- Undermining Critical Conversation: It is more difficult to have fruitful discussion and reach an agreement when facts are disputed or subjective.

Addressing the Epidemic of Misinformation:

- Media Literacy Education: In today's curricula, it is crucial to teach students how to assess sources, spot bias, and validate assertions.

- Platform Accountability: There is growing pressure on social media corporations to combat misinformation through algorithmic transparency, fact-checking collaborations, and content control.

- Independent Fact-Checkers: Although their reach is occasionally constrained in comparison to viral content, organizations such as PolitiFact, FactCheck.org, and Snopes are essential in dispelling myths.

Fighting false information is a cultural and pedagogical issue as much as a technical one. The first step in creating a more astute public is to provide people especially young students the skills and attitude necessary to inquire, confirm, and engage in critical thought.

4.4 Critical Analysis in the Google Age

The importance of how we think has perhaps outweighed what we know in a time when information can be found with a simple search. A fundamental talent for navigating the digital information ecosystem is the capacity for critical thought, which includes the ability to assess sources, analyze arguments, and synthesize knowledge.

The Effect of Google:

Externalization of Information: Search engines are increasingly being used by people to handle their memories. Rapid access is made possible by this, but deep learning and retention may suffer as a result.

- Simple comprehension: Search results skimming frequently results in cursory interaction with the material. The curiosity that motivates further in-depth investigation may be replaced by the ease of answers.

- Emergent Appreciation: The demand for quick fixes can erode tenacity and patience, two qualities necessary for thorough research and education.

Key Competencies for Critical Thinking in the Digital Age:

- Source Assessment: Assessing dependability requires knowing the information's publisher, their qualifications, and any potential biases.

- Analysis of Arguments: Dissecting an argument's claims, supporting details, and logic allows one to distinguish between sound reasoning and fallacies.

- The use of cross-referencing: Verifying information from several sources lowers the possibility of being duped.

The concept of contextual thinking Understanding a piece of information's larger historical, cultural, and political context gives it more depth and complexity.

Encouraging Critical Thinking in the Classroom:

- The use of inquiry-based learning Students'

intellectual curiosity and rigor are developed when they are encouraged to pose questions and look for answers.

- Project-Based Evaluation: Assessing pupils through projects and research encourages critical thinking and problem-solving skills rather than memorization.

- Cooperative Conversation: Students learn to express opinions, listen intently, and hone their thinking through organized debates and discussions.

- Metacognition, or thinking about one's own thinking, is fostered by encouraging students to reflect on their thought processes.

The paradox of the digital age is that, although information is more accessible than ever, there is also a greater obligation than ever to analyze it critically. In the age of abundant knowledge, critical thinking is a survival skill, not a luxury.

Because it provides previously unheard-of access,

flexibility, and opportunity, the internet has completely changed education and the way people consume knowledge. However, it also introduces complexity, including cognitive shortcuts, distraction, and false information that contradicts conventional learning paradigms. People need to move beyond passive consumption in order to properly traverse this new terrain. They need to take an active and critical role in their own intellectual growth. Either by becoming proficient in digital literacy, using top-notch e-learning resources, or cultivating critical thinking skills, the way forward is to enable people to not only access knowledge, but also understand and apply it with purpose and discernment

CHAPTER 5

HUMAN CONNECTION AND RELATIONSHIPS

The nature of human relationships has drastically changed in a world where digital contacts are shaping society more and more. Our strongest connections can now be woven together by swipes, likes, video calls, and emojis, when in the past, connection meant being physically close and interacting with people in person. Our capacity to connect has been enhanced by technology, but it has also brought forth complications that call into question the fundamentals of our interpersonal relationships. In-depth discussions of romance, family, friendship, and the occasionally disastrous effects of online cruelty are covered in this chapter, which explores the changing nature of relationships in the digital age.

5.1 The Development of Romantic Relationships and Online Dating

Courtship has changed since the introduction of dating apps. What used to be mostly made possible by social networks, connections within the community, or random meetings has evolved into an algorithm-driven procedure that can be accessed with a few screen touches.

The Evolution of Courtship

Conventional dating practices frequently entailed a gradual escalation meeting at social events, at work, or through mutual acquaintances. With a focus on brief bios and immediate visual appeal, modern dating apps have streamlined this process into a quick, image-based selection process.

The following are some of the main changes:

- Accessibility and scale: Potential partners can now be found worldwide, surpassing geographical boundaries.
- Algorithmic matchmaking: Sites make recommendations for compatible matches based on user preferences and behavior, which may help some users connect more effectively.
- Changes in communication style: People now

engage in more textual and asynchronous first encounters, which frees them from the strain of impromptu conversation and enables them to deliberately craft their personalities.

Online dating has the following benefits:

- Increased accessibility to a wider range of individuals and experiences
- Increased awareness of underrepresented groups (such as LGBTQ+ people)
- Flexibility for people with limited mobility or hectic schedules

Difficulties and criticisms:

- Commodification of people: People are frequently reduced to profiles that are evaluated in a matter of seconds due to the gamified swiping feature.
- Emotional detachment and ghosting: Too many options might result in superficial relationships that reduce empathy and responsibility.
- Safety concerns: Caution is necessary due to the possibility of scams, catfishing, or dangerous encounters.

The ambitions and fears of contemporary love are reflected in online dating. In an era where pixels form first impressions, it presents previously unheard-of chances for connection but also necessitates a rethink of how we establish intimacy and trust.

5.2 Family Relationships in the Age of the Internet

Previously centered on community activities and shared physical locations, family life today crosses with a digital environment that both unites and separates. Even though they may share a home, parents and kids have very different internet personas. Siblings can maintain their relationship across countries, but their isolated screen time runs the danger of causing them to drift apart in public areas.

Impact on the Relationships Between Parents and Children

Parenting digitally has become a full-time job. Parents are frequently left playing catch-up as kids get access to smartphones and social media at younger and younger ages.

Notable effects include:

- Change in authority: Kids can now verify their parents' information instantly. This calls into question established home knowledge hierarchies.
- Parental surveillance vs. independence: Discussions over privacy and trust have been triggered by tools such as social media monitoring, GPS tracking, and screen time applications.
- Role modeling: Parents who are screen addicts may unintentionally exhibit the same tendencies they condemn in their kids.

Digital Devices and Sibling Relationships

Technology can create tensions even though it makes enjoyable shared experiences possible, such as cooperative social media projects, multiplayer games, and streaming movies. Opportunities for bonding may be diminished by personalized digital ecosystems, where each sibling is engrossed in their own TikTok fad or YouTube rabbit hole.

Digital family life's advantages:

- Simple family memory sharing using chat groups, movies, and pictures
- Opportunities for distant communication when physically apart (e.g., video conversations with deployed parents or university-aged children)

Emerging concerns:

- Digital addiction: Excessive screen time can lead to disengagement, hurting emotional availability and family bonding.
- Disputes over screen time guidelines**: Generational differences and varying degrees of digital literacy frequently exacerbate conflict between parents and kids.

Proactive communication, respect for one another's digital limits, and a deliberate attempt to combine shared online experiences with offline time are all necessary to preserve familial intimacy in the digital age.

5.3 Social Connections and Friendship in a Digital Age

Long regarded as one of the most important networks of

support for mental health, friendships are changing as a result of our online interactions. From private forums and gaming servers to direct messages and memes, technology presents both new opportunities and challenges for fostering relationships.

In the connected age, friendship is being redefined.

Nowadays, proximity is no longer a barrier to friendship. Having a "best friend" that you have never met in person is totally conceivable. Online communities, especially around shared interests like gaming, fandoms, or artistic endeavors, often give profound emotional support.

Key ways that friendships are altered by digital life:

- Persistence of contact: Chat applications and notifications allow friends to stay in constant communication, even when they live far away.
- Curation of identity: People post polished highlights rather than real moments on social media, which promotes performance and may strain real friendships.
- Social comparison can lead to feelings of jealousy, anxiety, or self-doubt, particularly among teenagers.

Positive impacts:

- The establishment of various international networks and support networks for people living in remote or underprivileged areas
- Reconnecting with old friends is easier.

The following are obstacles to friendship quality:

- Deep discussion is being replaced by superficial involvement.
- Disagreement brought on by misconstrued remarks or texts; pressure to remain available or present online at all times

Meaningful relationships still require empathy, time commitment, and shared vulnerability qualities that likes and retweets cannot fully replicate even while digital platforms can broaden the breadth and reach of friendships.

5.4 Online harassment and cyberbullying

Cyberbullying and harassment are troubling undercurrents that lurk beneath the surface of internet connections. The anonymity and reach that facilitate connections also provide an environment that is conducive to cruelty.

Comprehending the Character of Cyberbullying

Traditional bullying and cyberbullying are different in a number of important ways:

- It tracks victims through their gadgets, making it impossible for them to flee by returning home.
- Amplification: Within minutes, harassment can spread like wildfire, reaching hundreds or thousands of people.
- Anonymity: The seeming security of concealing themselves behind a screen may encourage offenders.

The following are examples of cyberbullying:

- Threatening or derogatory communications
- Disseminating false information or photoshopped images; social banishment from online forums or group chats
- Doxxing, or the publication of private information; deepfakes or movies that have been altered

Psychological and Emotional Impact

- Victims frequently struggle with anxiety, despair, and low self-esteem.
- Academic or professional decline brought on by mental anguish; sleep difficulties and physical symptoms including headaches or nausea; and, in the worst situations, suicide thoughts or self-harm

The Function of Social Media and Platforms

Although technology corporations are somewhat responsible for content moderation, they cannot bear the entire load.

Successful mitigation techniques include:

- Education: Instilling ethical behavior, empathy, and digital citizenship in children at an early age.
- Reporting mechanisms: Users must be able to report abuse on platforms with ease and effectiveness.
- Involvement of parents and institutions: Workplaces, schools, and families must have clear policies in place to deal with online abuse.

In the end, there needs to be a culture change that promotes an environment of respect, accountability, and support while treating online violence with the same seriousness as abuse that occurs in the real world.

The way we parent, love, make friends, and even injure each other has changed as a result of the internet. Although it presents new complexity that calls into question the fundamentals of human interactions, it also provides significant instruments for connection. It is more important than ever to retain communication, empathy, and honesty in this digital age. Both online and offline, relationships need to be fostered with purpose, empathy, and a readiness to change without sacrificing our humanity.

CHAPTER 6

THE WORKPLACE AND THE INTERNET

The way we work, interact, and approach job growth has been completely changed by the internet. The nature of employment has changed over the last few decades due to the digital landscape, moving away from traditional office settings and toward more flexible, virtual models. In addition to discussing some of the ethical issues raised by these developments, this chapter examines the different ways that the internet has changed the workplace, from remote employment to the emergence of the gig economy.

6.1 Digital Collaboration and Remote Work

By the time the COVID-19 pandemic compelled millions of workers to work from home, the idea of remote work was not new. Yet, the epidemic hastened the adoption of digital collaboration tools and remote working, reinforcing the notion that productivity can be achieved without traditional office space.

The Evolution of Remote Work

- Before the internet: Telecommuting, often known as remote work, was far less common but did exist in some form prior to the internet. Remote work became increasingly practical with the development of computers and early internet technology. Although it was still considered a fringe option in the early 2000s, distant communication was made easier by email and early iterations of video conferencing software like Skype.

- After the internet boom: The quick development of the internet made working from home or other places simpler. Employees were able to work from almost any location with an internet connection thanks to tools like Google Docs, Slack, and Zoom that facilitate virtual meetings, real-time communication, and file sharing.

- Acceleration of pandemic: Many workers around the world adopted remote work as the norm during the COVID-19 pandemic, and businesses swiftly embraced tools like Zoom, Microsoft Teams, and

Slack. The changeover demonstrated the possibility of remote work, not just as a temporary fix, but as a sustainable, long-term option for many businesses.

Virtual Offices and Productivity Tools

- Cloud-based collaboration: Trello, Microsoft 365, Google Workspace, and other platforms have proven indispensable for digital collaboration, allowing teams to collaborate in real time, work on documents, and monitor projects from any place. Physical file storage has been supplanted by cloud storage, which facilitates information sharing and remote access.

- Project management and task tracking: Asana, Jira, and Monday.com are just a few of the tools that help teams and businesses keep organized and monitor the status of various assignments. By encouraging collaboration, these platforms make sure that everyone is in agreement and that projects proceed without hiccups.

- Difficulties of remote collaboration: Although remote work is convenient and flexible, it has also come with drawbacks, including the possibility of burnout because work and personal life are not kept separate, as well as communication or teamwork issues in groups that are not used to working remotely.

The Prospects for Remote Work

With some workers working from home and others attending offices, remote work is probably going to take a hybrid form in the future. Companies are increasingly embracing a paradigm in which workers are free to work from any location as long as they fulfill specific performance standards and deadlines. To guarantee that distant teams can work together effectively, businesses will also need to make investments in digital solutions that promote cooperation and team-building.

6.2 The Gig Economy and Job Creation

The gig economy's growth is one of the biggest changes to the contemporary workplace. In addition to opening up new career pathways, the internet has made it simpler for people to find contract jobs, freelance work, and temporary employment opportunities that weren't available only a few decades ago. Both employers and individuals now view work differently as a result of platforms like Fiverr, Uber, and Upwork.

The Gig Economy's Ascent

- Describe the gig economy. The phrase "gig economy" describes the increasing number of people working in flexible, short-time jobs that are frequently made possible via online platforms. These platforms link independent contractors with customers in need of certain services, such as site development, marketing, and food delivery and ride-sharing.

- Evolving perspectives on work: Many workers who are looking for flexibility find the gig economy appealing since it gives them greater control over their work schedules and locations. But there are drawbacks to this new paradigm as well, such as unstable employment, uneven compensation, and the lack of perks like retirement plans or health insurance.

- The function of the internet: The gig economy relies heavily on the internet, which offers platforms that link employers and employees. Professionals can locate freelance work in disciplines like writing, programming, design, and marketing through platforms like Upwork and Freelancer. While food delivery apps like DoorDash provide couriers with flexible gig work, ride-sharing services like Uber and Lyft have opened up new revenue streams for drivers.

Disrupting traditional employment

- Impact on Traditional Employment Models Conventional employment patterns have been upended by the gig economy's growth. Nowadays, a lot of people are choosing gig labor over full-time, permanent jobs. enterprises now hire, manage, and retain workers differently as a result of this transition, with more and more enterprises depending on contractors or freelancers to fill workforce gaps.

- Benefits and drawbacks for employees: Although the gig economy allows for more freedom, workers frequently encounter difficulties including inconsistent income and a dearth of benefits.

Financial instability results from the fact that many gig workers do not receive paid time off, retirement savings programs, or health insurance.

- Benefits and drawbacks for employers: Because companies are not required to provide benefits or long-term employment contracts, the gig economy can lower labor expenses for employers. However, there may be drawbacks, such as decreased employee loyalty, possible difficulties in overseeing a distributed staff, and problems with worker classification (e.g., independent contractor versus employee).

This is the gig economy's future. With more people choosing to work for themselves and businesses depending more and more on contractors, the gig economy is predicted to expand. However, when governments start to address the issues raised by this new labor paradigm, there can be requests for improved protections for gig workers, such as benefits and equitable pay.

6.3 Employee Autonomy, Monitoring, and Surveillance

Businesses now have more ways to keep an eye on their workers thanks to the internet, especially when they work remotely. Employers frequently defend surveillance as a means of boosting output and protecting data, but the practice raises serious ethical questions about employee autonomy and privacy.

Tools for Surveillance and Monitoring

- Software for Employee Monitoring: Employers are using a variety of techniques to keep an eye on employee activities as remote work has become more popular. These programs can monitor websites visited, record keystrokes, track how long employees spend on activities, and even take images of employees' desktops. Software such as Hubstaff, Time Doctor, and ActivTrak are a few examples.

- The following are the reasons to monitor: Employers contend that keeping an eye on staff members helps them stay productive, maintain security, and stop possible misbehavior. Surveillance can be viewed as essential to preventing breaches in sectors like healthcare and finance that handle sensitive data.

- The delicate distinction between incursion and

monitoring: On the other hand, overzealous monitoring might damage employee autonomy and trust. Constant employee monitoring can cause tension, anxiety, and mistrust, all of which can negatively impact the workplace as a whole.

Balancing Productivity and Privacy

- Ethical concerns: Monitoring may violate workers' right to privacy, which is an increasing worry. Many employees contend that they ought to be free to carry out their duties without feeling like they are being observed all the time. Businesses have a difficult time juggling the demands of productivity and security with the privacy of their employees.

- The balance of power has changed due to remote work, giving employees greater freedom to control their time. Greater job satisfaction and performance may result from this enhanced autonomy, but it also means that employers must have more faith in their staff and refrain from micromanaging them.

- Legal considerations: Businesses must make sure they adhere to local rules as different nations have different laws surrounding employee monitoring.

For example, the General Data Protection Regulation (GDPR) of the European Union imposes stringent restrictions on the gathering of personal information.

The Prospects for Employee Monitoring

Businesses will probably keep using increasingly complex monitoring technologies as technology develops. To make sure that surveillance doesn't violate people's privacy or autonomy, there might be more demands for openness, employee permission, and defined limitations.

6.4 The Dissolution of Work-Life Distinction

The merging of work and personal life is one of the biggest problems in the digital age. Even outside of office hours, it has been more challenging to completely unplug and disconnect from work due to the constant access to business emails, messages, and data.

The Difficulty of Constantly Being "On"

- Continuous Connectivity: In the age of the internet, people are constantly "on." Employees must always be accessible, whether via video calls, instant messaging, or email. People find it more difficult to distinguish between their personal and professional life as a result of this constant connectedness, which has blurred the boundaries between work and home.

- The effect on psychological well-being: Anxiety, worry, and burnout can result from an unwillingness to disconnect. Even when they are not formally on the clock, employees may feel as though they are working nonstop. Both work-life balance and general mental health may suffer as a result of this "always-on" society.

The Importance of Boundaries

- Setting boundaries: It is crucial for employers and employees to set clear boundaries in order to lessen the effects of constant connectedness. This can involve establishing clear guidelines for availability, restricting communication after hours, and designating certain "downtime" times during which staff members are urged to unplug from their job.

- Time management techniques: Time-blocking and "do not disturb" settings are two time management strategies that can help people better organize their workday and prevent overwork. People can recharge and preserve a good work-life balance by designating particular periods for personal pursuits like family time or exercise.

Work-Life Balance in the Future

- There will probably be a move toward more flexible work arrangements that enable employees to manage work and personal obligations as remote work grows in popularity.

- Obligations, both personal and professional. More comprehensive mental health care, such as mindfulness training, flexible scheduling, and improved support networks for workers who experience burnout, may potentially be a feature of the workplace of the future.

In addition to providing flexibility and convenience, the internet has fundamentally changed the workplace by posing new difficulties for both companies and employees. In order to ensure that both innovation and ethical considerations are at the forefront of workplace decisions, it is imperative that we carefully navigate the junction of technology as we move forward

CHAPTER 7

THE FUNCTION OF THE INTERNET IN SOCIAL TRANSFORMATION

The internet has developed into a potent instrument for social change, allowing people and organizations to organize movements, question the existing quo, and elevate underrepresented voices. The internet has changed the way we interact with social issues through citizen journalism, digital activism, and the international dissemination of ideas. But this authority also has drawbacks, such as concerns about freedom of speech, censorship, and the divisive nature of algorithmic material. This chapter explores the advantages and problems of the internet's significant influence on societal transformation.

7.1 Online Movements and Digital Activism

Digital activism has become one of the most powerful instruments for social change in recent years. Social justice movements have acquired international attention by using hashtags, viral campaigns, and internet petitions to reach people who might not otherwise be aware of important concerns. Social media serves as a mobilizing tool and a megaphone, allowing underrepresented voices and movements to thrive on the internet.

The Rise of Digital Activism

- The power of hashtags: Social issues have become worldwide movements thanks to the usage of hashtags like #MeToo, #BlackLivesMatter, and #ClimateStrike. In addition to coordinating protests, these digital tags have produced forums where individuals can express solidarity, share personal narratives, and call for change. For instance, #MeToo gained international recognition for sexual harassment and assault, enabling survivors to speak up about their experiences and hold influential people responsible.
- Viral campaigns and online petitions: Change.org petitions and other digital campaigns have pushed governments, businesses, and institutions to make big changes because they can quickly reach millions of people. These campaigns are frequently

spearheaded by activists, celebrities, and social media influencers, but they can also be started by regular people who recognize a problem and use online resources to advocate for change.

- Influencers on social media have emerged as important figures in influencing public opinion. They frequently draw attention to injustices, promote activism, and raise awareness of significant social issues via their platforms. Influencers with sizable fan bases have the power to inspire people to take action, whether it be by participating in protests or making charitable donations.

Case Studies of Effective Online Movements

- #MeToo: Initially conceived as a hashtag to increase awareness of the pervasiveness of sexual harassment and assault, the #MeToo movement swiftly expanded into a worldwide campaign. Millions of women (and men) shared their tales online, calling for responsibility and systemic change. Real-world implications of the movement included prominent people suffering from legal issues and career setbacks.

- #BlackLivesMatter: Black Lives Matter was founded in 2013 and gained traction following the horrific deaths of African Americans at the hands of law enforcement. The campaign and hashtag promoted ending institutional racism, reforming the police, and promoting justice. Black communities' voices were amplified and large-scale protests were coordinated globally thanks in large part to social media.

- Climate Action Movements: Greta Thunberg and other leaders in climate activism have mobilized young people online and pushed for legislative measures to address climate change. Thunberg started the #FridaysForFuture movement, which spread around the world and motivated millions of youth to demonstrate and demand that governments take immediate action on climate change.

Difficulties with Digital Activism

Despite its impressive achievements, digital activism still confronts obstacles. Trolls and critics may take over movements, and because social media is so ephemeral, momentum can soon fade if there isn't enough consistent participation. Online movements may also encounter opposition or be swayed by authorities or groups that aim to stifle dissent.

7.2 The Democratization of Media and Citizen Journalism

The emergence of the internet has made media production and delivery more accessible to all. The power dynamics of traditional media have changed as a result of citizen journalism, which is made possible by smartphones, social media, and blogging platforms. Nowadays, people can record events, disseminate news instantly, and offer alternate viewpoints that might not be heard in the media.

The Power of the People as Journalists

- Real-time reporting: People may now report on events as they happen thanks to social media sites like Facebook, Instagram, and Twitter. Bypassing the gatekeepers of traditional media, regular individuals on the ground during major events like protests, natural catastrophes, or political instability can now share their experiences with the globe.
- YouTube and Blogging: Individuals are now able to

produce and distribute content that questions established media channels thanks to websites like YouTube and personal blogs. In addition to providing viewpoints that mainstream media might miss, citizen journalists frequently create content that is more unvarnished, personal, and real.

- The role of social media in news dissemination: For many people, social media has supplanted traditional news channels as their main source of news, frequently breaking stories first. Social media is now used by news companies for real-time updates, citizen-generated material, and breaking news. As a result of this change, journalism has become more participatory, allowing readers to discuss, comment, and even question the material being reported.

The Advantages of Citizen Journalism

- Alternative perspectives: Citizen journalists frequently report on topics that the mainstream media overlooks or misrepresents, particularly those pertaining to social justice concerns, political dissidents, and neglected populations. These voices have raised awareness of issues like environmental justice, human rights abuses, and police brutality that were previously disregarded.

- Quality and ease of access: Particularly during events like protests or natural disasters, citizen journalism may quickly disseminate news to a worldwide audience. Bypassing the frequently slower reporting cycles of traditional media, people can submit first-hand stories, photos, and videos.

The Drawbacks of Citizen Journalism

- Bias and misinformation: Misinformation is another drawback of the widespread use of citizen-generated content. Without editorial control, biased content, rumors, and fake news can spread quickly. The credibility of citizen journalism may be weakened by a lack of professional journalistic standards or fact-checking.

- Accountability challenges: Editorial procedures, fact-checking, and legal supervision are how traditional media sources are held responsible for their news. However, citizen journalists frequently lack these protections, which could raise moral questions about truth, privacy, and sensationalism.

Citizen Journalism's Future

Citizen journalism will probably become even more important in forming global narratives as internet availability grows. To limit the hazards of misinformation, platforms and journalists will need to establish stronger procedures for verification and fact-checking.

7.3 Freedom of Expression and Internet Censorship

People now use the internet as a primary platform for sharing ideas, voicing opinions, and contesting authority. But as the digital world expands, so does the difficulty of speech regulation. The internet censorship practices of various nations have resulted in a complicated environment where control over online material and freedom of speech frequently conflict.

International Differences in Internet Regulation

- China's Great Firewall: China's widespread control over online material is among the most well-known instances of internet censorship. The Great Firewall is a tool used by the Chinese government to censor content that it considers politically sensitive or subversive and to prohibit access to specific websites, including social media sites like Facebook, Twitter, and YouTube. Other authoritarian governments attempting to exert control over digital environments have used this control system as a model.

- The Digital Policies of the European Union: In terms of digital space regulation, the European Union has taken the lead, especially with regard to privacy rules such as the General Data Protection Regulation (GDPR). The EU strives to strike a balance between free speech and laws that prohibit hate speech, online harassment, and disinformation, even as it places a strong emphasis on protecting privacy.

- The role of tech platforms in content moderation has come under scrutiny in the United States due to the controversy surrounding Section 230 of the Communications Decency Act. Platforms like Facebook, Twitter, and YouTube are shielded from liability for user-generated content by Section 230, but this legal protection has sparked calls for reform, especially in light of problems with hate speech, disinformation, and online radicalization.

Censorship's Ethical Implications

- Freedom vs. security: Governments frequently contend that censorship is required to uphold national security, stop terrorism, or stop online extremism. But this brings up the question of how to strike a balance between freedom of speech and security. For instance, censorship that targets political opposition can be an oppressive tactic that silences minority voices and stifles public discourse.

- Control of the corporation: A major part of content moderation is done by numerous big digital companies, such as Google and Facebook. Given that these private firms have considerable influence over what content is permitted to post on their platforms, this calls into question corporate control over free expression. Concern over the conflict between free speech and corporate interests is growing.

Internet Censorship's Future

Governments and tech corporations will have to deal with

the challenges of controlling online material as the internet develops further. Clear legislative frameworks, greater openness from internet platforms, and international cooperation will all be necessary to strike a balance between censorship and free speech.

7.4 Echo chambers and social polarization

Social polarization and echo chambers spaces where people are solely exposed to material that supports their own opinions have increased as a result of the proliferation of algorithm-driven content on social media.

How Algorithms Influence Public Conversation

- Personalized content: Social media companies employ algorithms to present material that is customized based on user interactions, browsing history, and preferences. Although this can increase the relevance of the content, there is a chance that it will reinforce preconceived notions. A fragmented and polarized internet environment results from users being less exposed to competing views or difficult information.

- Confirmation bias: The propensity to ignore contradicting facts and favor information that confirms one's opinions is reinforced by algorithms. This makes it more difficult for people to participate in productive, knowledgeable conversations by creating echo chambers where they are caught in a cycle of only seeing information that supports their opinions.

The Impact on Society

- Deepening divides: As people grow more firmly committed to their opinions and less open to discussing them, the polarization that echo chambers promote can exacerbate social divisions. Finding common ground on important topics may become more difficult as a result, which may exacerbate societal tensions, political polarization, and even extremism.

- Public discourse fragmentation: The potential for a common public conversation is threatened by the fragmentation of online platforms, as various groups create separate bubbles. Tribalism frequently takes precedence over sincere discussion of concepts and facts in public debates.

The Future of Social Polarization

With social media's continued influence debate, it will be crucial to make an effort to combat polarization. Initiatives to promote discourse across ideological divisions, media literacy training to assist consumers in critically assessing online content, and algorithmic changes that support a variety of viewpoints are among possible remedies.

Unquestionably, the internet has a significant impact on social change by democratizing media, providing previously unheard-of chances for activism, and combating censorship. But there are also serious drawbacks, such as the proliferation of false information, escalating polarization, and the moral difficulties of speech regulation. Finding a balance that safeguards free speech while making sure the internet continues to be a force for good in advancing social justice and constructive change is crucial as we continue to traverse the digital terrain

CHAPTER 8

SECURITY, PRIVACY, AND ETHICAL ISSUES

Our lives are becoming more and more entwined with the internet world in the current digital era. Our activities, preferences, and interactions are gathered, processed, and stored in an ever-expanding digital ecosystem from the time we wake up until we go to sleep. Significant breakthroughs have been made possible by this convenience, but it has also raised serious ethical, security, and privacy issues. The difficulties of safeguarding private data, maintaining online safety, and setting moral limits are all growing as the internet does. These important subjects are examined in this chapter, with particular attention paid to the importance of personal information, the escalating risks to cybersecurity, the moral conundrums raised by surveillance technology, and the development of a digitally responsible culture.

8.1 Personal Information: The Internet Age's Currency

In the current digital economy, personal data has become a valuable commodity. Businesses, governments, and other organizations use the enormous volumes of data we produce online to target advertising, build comprehensive user profiles, and support business models. However, significant concerns over control and privacy are brought up by the extensive gathering and commercialization of this data.

The Data Monetization Process

Businesses can benefit greatly from personal data, which includes details about our location, purchasing choices, surfing patterns, and even private conversations. Data firms frequently use this information to create recommendations and ads that are tailored to each individual, which boosts sales and enhances customer interaction. However, the user may not always be able to see the whole cost of these services. We may receive "free" apps, social networking sites, and internet services, but in the background, our personal information is being gathered and turned into a commodity.

- Data Brokers: A mostly unseen aspect of the digital economy, data brokers collect, analyze, and sell user data to the highest bidder. These businesses have access to a wealth of data, including personal health information, political affiliations, buying habits, and credit scores. Following that, this information may be utilized for profiling, targeted marketing, or even more sinister uses like identity theft.

- Social Media Platforms and Ad Revenue: By gathering user data to target ads, social media behemoths like Facebook, Instagram, and Google make billions of dollars. These platforms are able to provide us with individualized material that keeps us interested for longer since they know more about us than many of our closest friends. Our data is one of these businesses' most precious assets as the more information they can gather, the more successful their ads will be.

The Repercussions of Data Exploitation

Despite the obvious financial usefulness of personal data, gathering it has a number of concerns. Data breaches have the potential to reveal private information, which can lead to identity theft, monetary loss, and harm to one's reputation. The sheer volume of personal information that businesses gather and keep makes them an alluring target for hackers, even in the absence of any immediate harm.

Concerns over surveillance capitalism are also raised by the collection of personal data. As individuals, we frequently have little control over how our data is utilized and may not always completely comprehend it. It can be challenging for customers to understand what they're agreeing to when they accept the lengthy and complicated terms of service found on many digital platforms.

Taking Charge of Personal Information

Globally, privacy regulations are being implemented to address these problems. Strict rules on how businesses can gather, keep, and utilize personal data are outlined in the European Union's General Data Protection Regulation (GDPR). Users have the right to view, update, and remove their personal information from platforms thanks to these legislation.

Nevertheless, businesses continue to discover ways to get around laws in spite of these legal actions, and data privacy is still a major problem for anyone using the internet. Users must be more watchful, knowledgeable about their rights, and aware of the resources available to protect their data if they want to take control of it.

8.2 Digital Vulnerabilities and Cybersecurity Risks

The risks that endanger our online safety are growing along with the internet. Cybersecurity has emerged as a critical issue for governments, corporations, and individuals alike. The digital world is full of flaws that can lead to extensive damage, from ransomware assaults to data breaches.

Typical Cybersecurity Risks

Cyber threats are constantly changing, and being aware of the different kinds of risks we encounter is essential to being safe online. Among the most frequent dangers are:

- Phishing attacks are fraudulent emails or texts that deceive people into disclosing private information, such bank account information or passwords.

Phishing scams are especially harmful because they frequently mimic authentic emails from banks or well-known internet businesses.

- Ransomware: This malicious software encrypts files or locks users out of their systems and demands a fee to unlock them. Hospitals, schools, and even entire cities have been the targets of ransomware attacks, which have seriously disrupted operations.

- Data Breaches: In order to obtain private user information, hackers frequently target big businesses, governmental agencies, and financial institutions. Users may be vulnerable to fraud and identity theft as a result of these breaches, which may reveal private data including passwords, addresses, and credit card numbers.

- Malware: Any software intended to damage or take advantage of a computer system is considered malware. These include Trojan horses, worms, and viruses that can corrupt files, steal data, or take over systems.

The Development of Internet Safety

As cyber dangers have become increasingly complex, so

too have the defenses against them. Online safety precautions have changed throughout time, and security technologies like multi-factor authentication (MFA), encryption, and firewalls are now crucial parts of electronic defense.

- Encryption: This method makes sure that private data, such credit card numbers or private messages, is jumbled and unintelligible to anybody without the right decryption key. The encryption of secure websites (those that utilize HTTPS) makes it more difficult for hackers to intercept data while it is being transmitted.

- Antivirus and Anti-Malware Software: These applications identify, block, and remove harmful software from computers. Updating software is essential in the battle against changing cyberthreats.

- Multi-Factor Authentication (MFA): This security feature asks users to produce multiple pieces of proof to confirm their identity, like a mobile device verification code or a password and fingerprint. A further line of defense against hacking attempts is provided by MFA.

Notwithstanding these developments, cybersecurity risks continue to be a dynamic problem. It is crucial for people and companies to keep aware of new dangers and implement the most recent security procedures since cybercriminals are always coming up with new ways to get around security measures.

8.3 Surveillance Technologies' Ethical Conundrums

The distinction between privacy and safety has gotten more hazy with the introduction of sophisticated surveillance technology like facial recognition and predictive policing. Although these technologies have a lot to offer in terms of public safety and crime prevention, they also bring up serious ethical issues about civil liberties, privacy, and the possibility of misuse.

Technologies for Facial Recognition

One of the most contentious surveillance technologies available today is facial recognition. Law enforcement organizations frequently use technology to track and identify people in real time, frequently in public areas like malls, airports, and even city streets. Although it can be a helpful tool for tracking down missing people or criminals, there are serious privacy dangers involved.

- Mass surveillance: Authorities can monitor entire populations without consent by using facial recognition technology for mass surveillance. This prompts worries about the expansion of governmental power and the degradation of personal liberties.
- Research has indicated that facial recognition systems are susceptible to bias, especially in the areas of racial and gender profiling. It has been discovered that these algorithms misidentify women and persons of color more frequently than white men, which could result in prejudice and unfairness.

The use of predictive policing

Algorithms are used in predictive policing to evaluate data and forecast crime hot spots. Law enforcement organizations are able to more efficiently distribute resources as a result. But there are worries about biases being reinforced because of the dependence on past data.

- Bias and discrimination: Historical crime data, which predictive police systems frequently use, may reveal historical policing biases, such as the disproportionate targeting of minority communities. Racial and socioeconomic disparities may worsen as a result, and a cycle of excessive policing may be sustained.

- Transparency and accountability: A large number of predictive police algorithms are proprietary, which means they are not accessible to the general public or transparent. These technologies run the possibility of being utilized in ways that infringe on citizens' rights if there is no control.

Ethical Limits of Monitoring

Individual rights must be properly balanced with the use of surveillance technologies. Any technology that violates the fundamental human right to privacy needs to be carefully examined for ethical issues. Organizations and governments should make sure that surveillance procedures are open, responsible, and subject to impartial review.

8.4 Fostering a Digitally Responsible Culture

The need for people, businesses, and governments to embrace a culture of digital responsibility is growing along with the digital world. Understanding the effects of our online behavior and making deliberate choices that support moral, secure, and civil interactions are key components of digital responsibility.

The Role of Education

- Digital literacy: To help people use the internet in a responsible and safe manner, digital literacy instruction is crucial. Digital literacy gives people the skills they need to make wise decisions, from identifying online hazards to comprehending how personal data is gathered.

- Privacy awareness: People ought to be informed about their rights with regard to personal information and how to guard against abuse. Users can take charge of their information with the support of awareness campaigns and unambiguous privacy policies.

Business Accountability

Businesses have a significant influence on how the digital world is shaped. They have to be open and honest about how they gather, utilize, and safeguard user data. They should also give user privacy top priority in product design and make significant investments in security measures to thwart cyberattacks.

Accountability of the Government

Governments are required to control the use of surveillance technologies and guarantee the protection of citizens' right to privacy. In the digital age, robust laws and regulations like the GDPR offer a foundation for data protection and freedom preservation.

Encouraging Responsible Online Behavior

- Ethical decision-making: We all have a responsibility to think about the moral ramifications of the things we do online. Each of us has an obligation to maintain moral principles in the digital sphere, from protecting privacy to having constructive social conversations.

- Respect and online etiquette: Building a more responsible and compassionate online culture involves avoiding negative behaviors like cyberbullying, respecting others' privacy, and having meaningful interactions.

It is impossible to overestimate the significance of privacy, security, and ethics as digital technologies develop further. We can guarantee that the internet stays a secure and moral place for everyone by tackling these issues, encouraging greater transparency, and cultivating a culture of responsibility

CHAPTER 9

THE HUMAN BODY, LIFESTYLE, AND HEALTH

Never before has the relationship between technology and healthcare been so obvious. Our perspective on health and fitness has drastically changed with the onset of the digital age. Wearable technology, online support groups, and digital connectivity are changing how we track, preserve, and enhance our mental and physical well-being. Even while technology has made amazing strides, there are risks and difficulties that need to be carefully considered. Examining the emergence of telemedicine, the function of wearable technology, the effects of sedentary lifestyles, and the influence of online health groups, this chapter explores how health and lifestyle are changing in the digital era.

9.1 The Development of Virtual Health Services and Telemedicine

Healthcare used to be mostly provided by in-person visits

to clinics, hospitals, and doctor's offices. However, telemedicine and virtual consultations have become increasingly prevalent in the healthcare sector in recent years, altering how people communicate with medical professionals. In an era of rapid digital transformation, the opportunity to consult with a doctor or specialist from the comfort of one's home has created new opportunities for the delivery of healthcare.

Telemedicine: A Revolution in Healthcare Access

Telemedicine refers to the use of digital communication tools, such as video conferencing, mobile apps, and messaging platforms, to provide healthcare services remotely. Geographical constraints that formerly restricted access to healthcare have been removed because of this innovation, which enables people to receive care from almost anywhere. People in underserved or rural areas, where there are few healthcare practitioners, have benefited most from it.

- Convenience: Patients can now obtain medical advice more easily without having to travel or take time off work thanks to virtual consultations. It works well for follow-up visits, minor medical issues, and mental health assistance.

- Cost-Effective: Telemedicine can lower the expenses of in-person appointments, including transportation, missed work, and facility overhead, for both patients and healthcare systems.

- Changed Scope: When traditional healthcare visits were restricted by lockdowns and social distancing measures during public health emergencies like the COVID-19 epidemic, telemedicine proved to be extremely helpful. It has reduced the danger of infection while enabling healthcare systems to continue operating.

Telemedicine's Limitations

Telemedicine has transformed healthcare, but it has drawbacks as well. Hands-on examination, diagnostic testing, or the use of medical equipment are necessary for certain illnesses or health difficulties that cannot be recreated on a computer. For example, in-person visits are still necessary for physical examinations, blood tests, and imaging procedures like MRIs and X-rays. Additionally, internet connectivity is essential to the efficacy of virtual consultations, which could be a deterrent for those living in rural or low-income locations.

Notwithstanding these obstacles, the field of telemedicine is expanding quickly and has great promise for raising the effectiveness and accessibility of healthcare services globally. Telemedicine will probably continue to develop as technology does, utilizing artificial intelligence and increasingly complex diagnostic tools to improve the standard of care.

9.2 Health Tracking and Wearables: A New Age of Self-Monitoring

A new era of self-monitoring and personal health management has been brought about by the development of wearable technology. Smartwatches, fitness trackers, and biofeedback technologies have given people unprecedented control over their health. Numerous physical health metrics, including heart rate, activity level, sleep patterns, and even blood oxygen levels, are continuously recorded by these devices.

The Contribution of Wearable Technology to Wellness Promotion

Wearable technology, especially smartwatches and fitness trackers, has become essential for tracking and enhancing health. These gadgets have sensors that monitor users' daily activities, motivating them to lead healthier lives, stay active, and get better sleep.

- Fitness Tracking: Track your steps, calories burnt, and exercises using devices like Fitbit, Garmin, and Apple Watch. People are inspired to continue active and reach their fitness objectives by this continuous feedback.

- Health Metrics Monitoring: In addition to measuring basic fitness, many wearables can measure more complex health metrics including blood oxygen levels, heart rate variability, and ECG readings. By warning users of possible health problems like irregular heartbeats or low oxygen levels, these technologies can encourage people to seek medical help if needed.

- Sleep Tracking: Wearable technology has made it simpler to monitor the length and quality of sleep, which is important for general health. Users can learn more about their sleep patterns and make changes to enhance rest and recuperation by tracking variables including heart rate, movement, and REM sleep cycles.

Mental Health and Biofeedback

Through biofeedback technologies that measure physiological responses like heart rate, skin temperature, and sweat levels, wearables are also being utilized to monitor mental health. Users can learn more about how their bodies react to stress, anxiety, and other emotional stimuli by using these gadgets.

- Stress Management: Wearables can give consumers real-time feedback on how their bodies are reacting to stresses by monitoring physiological markers of stress. People can use this information to practice deep breathing, mindfulness, and other stress-reduction methods.
- Mental Health Insights: People can learn more about how their lifestyle affects their mental health by using devices that measure their stress levels,

physical activity, and sleep patterns. People may seek professional assistance if they experience symptoms of anxiety or sadness, such as a decline in physical activity or poor sleep quality.

The Wearables' Privacy Issues

Wearables present issues regarding data privacy even though they have amazing advantages for self-monitoring and health optimization. Sensitive health data is continuously gathered by these devices and is frequently shared with outside organizations for study or stored on cloud servers.

- Data Ownership: Concerns about who controls the data produced by wearables and its usage are becoming more and more significant. It is important for users to understand how their data is being used and whether it is being shared with researchers, advertising, or other outside parties.
- Security Risks: Wearables are susceptible to hacking and data breaches, just like any other digital instrument. Identity theft, insurance fraud, or discrimination based on health information may

result from compromised health data.

Notwithstanding these reservations, wearable technology represents a major breakthrough in personal health tracking, enabling people to take charge of their health and identify possible problems early.

9.3 Internet-Induced Health Problems and Sedentary Lifestyles

While there are many advantages to the digital revolution, sedentary lifestyles are becoming a bigger public health concern. Many people are spending more time sitting than ever before as a result of their growing reliance on digital devices for socializing, entertainment, and work. Numerous health concerns, such as obesity, heart disease, and musculoskeletal disorders, have increased as a result of this behavioral change.

How Screen Time Affects Physical Health

The increase in screen time is one of the main causes of sedentary lifestyles. Many people are sitting for extended amounts of time using displays, whether they be televisions, laptops, or cellphones. This behavior's physical costs are becoming more and more obvious.

- Obesity and Weight Gain: Lack of physical exercise is a major risk factor for obesity and is frequently brought on by a sedentary lifestyle. Long periods of sitting lower calorie expenditure, which increases the risk of obesity-related diseases such diabetes, high blood pressure, and heart disease as well as causes weight gain.

- Long-term sitting can lead to a number of musculoskeletal problems, such as poor posture, neck stiffness, and back pain. This is especially true for people who work at desks or do screen-based activities for extended periods of time.

- Cardiovascular Risk: Long periods of sitting have been linked to poor heart health, according to research. Inactivity lowers circulation and raises the risk of diseases including heart disease and high blood pressure. Sitting for the remainder of the day puts anyone at risk, including those who routinely work out.

Methods to Address Sedentary Conduct

It takes both awareness and activity to counteract the detrimental effects of a sedentary lifestyle. The following techniques can help reduce the dangers of extended sitting:

- Take Regular Breaks: You can lessen the hazards of extended sitting by setting reminders to stand, stretch, or walk every 30 to 60 minutes. Stretching and strolling about the room are easy ways to increase circulation and reduce tense muscles.
- The strain that bad posture exerts on the body can be lessened by making sure that workstations are ergonomically constructed. Standing desks, movable chairs, and strategically positioned screens can all significantly lessen musculoskeletal pain.
- The sedentary character of modern living can be countered by incorporating more physical activity into everyday activities, such as walking, cycling, or taking fitness courses.

People can lessen the negative health effects linked to sedentary behavior by embracing healthy behaviors and exercising mindfulness when using screens.

9.4 Support Networks and Online Health Communities

The digital era has changed how we engage with people about our health experiences as well as how we keep track of our health. For those looking for information, emotional support, and guidance on a variety of health-related topics, online health forums and support networks have grown to be indispensable tools.

Digital Health Communities' Power

People can share their experiences and gain knowledge from others through online forums, social media groups, and patient advocacy websites. People with uncommon diseases, mental health issues, or chronic problems often discover others who genuinely understand their struggles in these networks, which is especially helpful.

- Health Education: Online forums are a great way to learn about particular illnesses, therapies, and lifestyle modifications. Patients frequently offer their own experiences, study results, and suggestions, which can encourage others to take charge of their own health.

- Emotional Support: Online networks offer a sense of community and belonging, whereas health conditions can be isolating. Making connections with people who are experiencing comparable things might provide consolation and support on an emotional level.

- Peer-Led Initiatives: A lot of online health communities have started self-help or peer-led support programs where people can connect individually or in small groups to give emotional support, share coping mechanisms, and offer advice.

Difficulties and Hazards of Virtual Health Communities

Online health communities include risks, even if they offer many advantages. The dissemination, since not all of the material provided on these platforms is reliable or supported by proof, the spread of false information is a major worry.

- Misinformation: If people depend on unreliable or inaccurate health advice to make medical decisions, it can be detrimental. Users must consult medical experts to confirm the information they obtain from these platforms.

- The sharing of private health information in online groups presents privacy concerns. Some people could be discouraged from actively participating in discussions because many platforms do not guarantee complete confidentiality.

Online health communities are essential for promoting peer support, emotional wellness, and health literacy despite these hazards, particularly for people with chronic or uncommon medical illnesses.

Our approach to health and wellbeing has been profoundly changed by the digital revolution. Technology is changing how we track, maintain, and enhance our health, from wearables and telemedicine to the rise in sedentary lives and online health groups. Although these developments result in improvements, they also raise new issues and concerns. People must carefully traverse the terrain of digital health, striking a balance between the advantages of technology and the demands of privacy, exercise, and self-care. The future of health will become more personalized, accessible, and linked as we continue to adopt these advancements

CHAPTER 10

THE FUTURE OF HUMAN LIFE IN THE DIGITAL AGE

Nearly every element of human life has changed due to the quick development of technology, which has produced a digital environment in which we depend more and more on digital tools, immersive virtual worlds, and artificial intelligence (AI). These technologies are changing what it means to be human, not just improving our capacities. The significant ramifications of these developments necessitate careful thought as we stand on the brink of the digital future. This chapter will examine four major topics that will shape human existence in the digital age: virtual reality and the redefining of experience; artificial intelligence and human dependence; ethical frontiers such as transhumanism and digital immortality; and the goal of creating a sustainable digital society.

10.1 Human Dependency and Artificial Intelligence

Artificial intelligence's introduction into our daily lives has had a profoundly revolutionary impact. AI is becoming more and more integrated into our daily lives, from voice assistants like Siri and Alexa to driverless cars and AI-powered medical treatments. AI raises significant concerns regarding human dependence even as it offers previously unheard-of levels of efficiency and ease.

Convenience and Efficiency Driven by AI

By automating traditionally labor-intensive and time-consuming operations, artificial intelligence is transforming entire sectors. By managing repetitive jobs like data input, analysis, and customer service, artificial intelligence (AI) solutions are increasing efficiency in the workplace. AI algorithms are utilized in healthcare to provide individualized therapy recommendations and make accurate disease diagnoses. Everything from temperature control to security is made easier by smart home appliances that learn and adjust to our preferences.

- Workplace Efficiency: Automation powered by AI is increasing productivity across a range of industries, cutting down on errors and facilitating quicker decision-making. Employees can concentrate on more strategic and creative work by automating administrative activities, which boosts productivity overall.

- Healthcare Advancements: AI-powered diagnostic technologies can spot trends in medical data that human doctors would miss, enhancing treatment outcomes and early diagnosis. In several domains, like predictive analytics and medical imaging, AI is already surpassing humans.

- AI is included into the infrastructure of contemporary smart cities and houses. Everyday living is becoming more connected and efficient thanks to technology, from AI-powered appliances that adapt to your requirements to traffic management systems that optimize commuter routes.

The Dependency Shadow

Concern over humanity's growing reliance on AI systems is growing in spite of these advantages. The increasing prevalence of AI raises concerns regarding human capabilities, autonomy, and control. Will we lose our sense of purpose or ability to think critically if machines take over the majority of the work that humans used to perform? If we depend too much on algorithms, can we still make decisions on our own?

- Over-reliance on Technology: People may become reliant on AI systems for even simple decisions as these systems take over more decision-making tasks. For instance, people may follow directions mindlessly without taking into account the larger context, such as traffic conditions or safety, if navigation programs provide the quickest route. identical to this, AI-driven recommendation systems in commerce or entertainment might limit a person's originality and personal exploration by continuously recommending identical content.

- Skill Degradation: People run the risk of losing critical skills as AI continues to perform tasks that were previously completed by humans. The more we rely on robots to do jobs for us, from simple math to complex problem-solving, the more we risk forgetting how to do them ourselves. People may get so dependent on the digital world that they are unable to function outside of it.

- Privacy concerns are becoming more and more of a problem as AI systems handle everything from shopping habits to personal data. There is genuine concern that the likelihood of personal data being misused or exploited will rise in tandem with our increased reliance on AI.

In the future, it will be necessary to carefully manage the balance between human independence and AI-driven convenience. Although AI has great potential to improve people's lives, we must be careful that it doesn't erode our independence or lead to harmful dependences.

10.2 Virtual Reality and Experience Redefinition

These days, augmented reality (AR) and virtual reality (VR) are not just science fiction. The way we view and engage with the world is already being redefined by these immersive technologies. The boundaries between the real and virtual worlds are becoming increasingly hazy in the digital age, opening up previously unthinkable experiences.

Human Perception and Immersion Technologies

While augmented reality superimposes digital data on the actual world, virtual reality immerses viewers in simulated situations. When combined, these technologies are transforming how we connect with the world around us and bringing forth new kinds of social interaction, education, and entertainment.

- Entertainment and Gaming: One of the most well-known uses of virtual reality is in the gaming sector, where users can explore whole 3D environments with unrestricted mobility. With the advent of virtual reality (VR) gaming, users may enter their preferred virtual worlds with a level of immersion that is unmatched by conventional gaming mediums.

- Education and Training: By establishing immersive learning environments, VR and AR are transforming education. Without ever leaving the classroom, students can visit distant nations, tour historical landmarks, or take part in mock lab activities. In order to rehearse difficult procedures or scenarios in a safe and controlled environment, medical professionals, pilots, and military personnel are using virtual reality (VR) for simulation-based training.

- Social Interaction: Virtual reality is transforming social interactions in a world that depends more and more on digital connections. People can interact, meet, and work together in virtual places in ways that are not limited by geography. The capacity to participate in shared experiences is changing the fundamental structure of social relationships, as seen in social VR platforms like VRChat and virtual conferences.

Redefining Reality

The potential to completely alter human perception is enormous as VR and AR technology advance. Beyond just providing amusement, these technologies have the power to change our perceptions of who we are, how we interact with others, and even how we relate to reality itself.

- Identity and Presence: Since users can design avatars in virtual reality that embody their ideal selves, identity can be explored in ways that aren't feasible in the real world. Interesting queries concerning the nature of the self and the distinctions between digital and physical reality are brought up by this capacity to assume several personas.

- The psychological effects of prolonged VR use are a concern, despite the potential advantages of immersive experiences, such as offering an escape for individuals coping with stress or trauma. Being able to live in a virtual world could cause one to become disconnected from reality or increase feelings of loneliness.

- Blurred Boundaries: As VR and AR advance, it will probably become more difficult to distinguish between the real and virtual worlds. This calls into question how we evaluate relationships that take place in digital settings and how authentic encounters are.

In the end, the emergence of virtual reality holds the potential to fundamentally alter the human experience, presenting both thrilling possibilities and formidable obstacles.

10.3 Ethical Frontiers: Digital Immortality and Transhumanism

Many ethical conundrums are being brought about by the digital age, especially in the areas of digital immortality and transhumanism. The line between human biology from artificial enhancement is becoming increasingly blurred as technology develops. These hypothetical scenarios cast doubt on our basic conceptions of life, death, and humanity.

Transhumanism: Improving Human Capabilities

The belief that people can and ought to use technology to overcome their biological limits is known as transhumanism. Prosthetics and exoskeletons can be used to improve physical capabilities, and brain-computer interfaces (BCIs) can be used to enhance cognitive capacities. The objective is to transcend the constraints of nature so that people can live longer, healthier, and more capable lives.

- Physical Enhancement: Humans can already improve their physical capabilities thanks to biotechnology advancements like gene editing and prostheses. Transhumanist technologies are expanding the capabilities of the human body, from prosthetic limbs to sophisticated exoskeletons that enable people with disabilities to move around.

- Cognitive Augmentation: Direct contact between the brain and digital equipment is made possible by brain-computer interfaces, which may lead to improvements in cognitive function. These technologies may improve learning ability, memory, or even allow for psychic connection. But where do we draw the line between natural evolution and human intervention, and how much improvement is too much?

Digital Immortality: Existing in the Machine indefinitely

The concept of "digital immortality" refers to the

possibility that a person's mind could one day be implanted into a machine, enabling them to continue to exist after their physical body has died. The idea that human consciousness could be permanently stored in a computer format is known as mind uploading or whole brain emulation.

- Ethical Implications: There are significant ethical concerns with the concept of digital immortality. Since the human experience of life and death is irrevocably changed, is it really moral to implant consciousness into a machine? Would a digital version of a person only be a replica of their original awareness, or would the core of their identity be preserved?

- Inequality and Access: The possibility of digital immortality could lead to serious inequality. What would happen to society if only the powerful or wealthy could attain digital immortality, and who would have access to such technology? The idea also calls into question the essence of human identity—if we may live forever in a machine, what does it mean to be human?

It is crucial to take into account both the concepts' technical viability and the significant ethical concerns they raise for humanity's future as we continue to explore the fields of transhumanism and digital immortality.

10.4 Creating a Digital Society That Is Sustainable

It is crucial to consider how we might create a society that is both sustainable and compassionate as we go further in the digital era. While there are many advantages to the digital revolution, there are drawbacks as well, including issues with inequality, privacy, security, and environmental sustainability.

Developing a Digital Future That Is Inclusive

Inclusion is one of the main objectives of a sustainable digital society. A gap between those who have access to digital resources and those who do not could be exacerbated by technological advancements. Investments in infrastructure, education, and technological access for all societal members—regardless of socioeconomic background or geographic location will be necessary to close this digital divide.

- Universal Access to Technology: One of the most important steps in creating a more inclusive digital society is making sure that everyone has access to the internet, digital tools, and educational materials. We can create more equal chances for growth and development by equipping underrepresented communities with the knowledge and resources they need to navigate the digital world.

- Digital Literacy: In a world when technology is everywhere, digital literacy is essential. Fostering a society that can effectively utilize the potential of digital technology requires teaching people not only how to use digital tools but also how to critically evaluate information, preserve their privacy, and traverse online settings safely.

Ethical Issues in the Development of Technology

- It is critical that we approach technological development with a solid ethical foundation as we create a digital society. Careful control and oversight will be necessary to ensure that technology benefits mankind rather than exploits it, due to issues with privacy and AI ethics.

- Privacy Protection: One of the most important issues in the digital age is data privacy. Strong regulatory frameworks and technology solutions that put user consent and data protection first will be necessary to create a society that values individual privacy while still utilizing digital innovation.

Impact on the Environment:

We must take into account the environmental impact of digital technologies as we adopt them. Sustainability must be a key factor in the creation of new technologies, from the energy usage of data centers to the garbage produced by electronic devices.

Digital Economies That Are Sustainable

An equitable and ecologically conscious digital economy is

also necessary for a sustainable digital society. Digital technologies must be incorporated into the global economy in ways that advance equity, lessen inequality, and provide long-term prosperity as they develop further.

In conclusion, there is a lot of promise for human life in the digital age, but it also necessitates responsible conduct and deliberate thought. We can build a digital future that is not just inventive and efficient but also sustainable and inclusive for everybody if we embrace technology breakthroughs while keeping an eye on human values and ethical standards.

ABOUT THE AUTHOR

Jaxon Vale, who specializes in AI-driven tactics that enable people to create scalable enterprises, is an ardent supporter of the nexus between technology and entrepreneurship. Jaxon has been in the vanguard of using artificial intelligence for creative and commercial endeavors, having a background in digital transformation, data science, and machine learning.

Jaxon has offered advice on how to use AI to advance oneself, make money from digital abilities, and expand side projects into successful companies over the years. Jaxon has worked with innumerable budding entrepreneurs, offering them tools, methods, and tips for success in the digital age. He has a natural curiosity and a dedication to helping others achieve.

When not working in the fields of artificial intelligence and business development, Jaxon likes to experiment with new technologies, produce creative digital content, and coach people on how to succeed in the rapidly evolving world of tech-driven opportunities.